Learn to Draw Manga

MANGA DINOSAURS

Illustrated by
Richard Jones & Jorge Santillan

PowerKiDS
press

New York

Published in 2013 by The Rosen Publishing Group, Inc.
29 East 21st Street, New York, NY 10010

First Edition

Produced for Rosen by Calcium Creative Ltd
Editor: Sarah Eason
Editor for Rosen: Sara Antill
Book Design: Paul Myerscough

Illustrations by Richard Jones and Jorge Santillan

Library of Congress Cataloging-in-Publication Data

Jones, Richard, 1979–
 Manga Dinosaurs / by Richard Jones & Jorge Santillan. — 1st ed.
    p. cm. — (Learn to draw manga)
 Includes index.
 ISBN 978-1-4488-7873-4 (library binding) —
ISBN 978-1-4488-7944-1 (pbk.) — ISBN 978-1-4488-7950-2 (6-pack)
1. Dinosaurs in art—Juvenile literature. 2. Comic books, strips,
etc.—Japan—Technique—Juvenile literature. 3. Drawing—
Technique—Juvenile literature. I. Santillan, Jorge. II. Title.
 NC1764.8.D56J66 2013
 741.5'1—dc23

                          2011052869

Manufactured in the United States of America

CPSIA Compliance Information: Batch #B4S12PK: For Further Information contact Rosen Publishing, New York, New York at 1-800-237-9932

Contents

Drawing Manga Dinosaurs   4

Brachiosaurus   6

Eoraptor   8

Hadrosaur   12

Tyrannosaurus rex   14

Stegosaurus   18

Deinonychus   20

Megalosaurus   24

More Dinosaurs   28

Glossary   30

Further Reading   31

Websites   31

Index   32

Drawing Manga Dinosaurs

"Manga" is a Japanese word that means "comic." Manga cartoons are famous around the world for their cool look and exciting characters. Now you can learn to draw amazing Manga figures yourself!

Manga gets prehistoric!

In this book, we are going to show you how to draw the most exciting dinosaurs to ever roam the planet, Manga-style!

4

You will need

To create your Manga dinosaurs, you will need some equipment:

Sketchpad or paper

Try to use good quality paper from an art store.

Pencils

A set of good drawing pencils are key to creating great character drawings.

Eraser

Use this to remove any unwanted lines.

Paintbrush, paints, and pens

The final stage for all your drawings will be to add color. We have used paints to complete the Manga dinosaurs in this book. If you prefer, you could use pens.

Brachiosaurus

This enormous giant grew up to 85 feet (26 m) long from head to tail. This was no flesh-eating monster, though. Brachiosaurs were plant-eating beasts.

Step 1

Draw a large oval for the body and cone shapes for the legs. Add the neck, head, and tail.

Step 2

Pencil some detail. Draw claws on the feet and add muscle lines to the body. Pencil the eyes, nostrils, and horns on the head.

Step 3

Add further detail with more muscle lines. Add shading to the body, neck, tail, and eyes.

Step 4

No one knows for sure what colors dinosaurs were. You could choose a pale green for the body with touches of bright blue elsewhere.

Eoraptor

This dinosaur's name means "morning plunderer." The meat-eating hunter moved quickly to attack prey with its razor-sharp claws and teeth.

Step 1

Give your dinosaur a leaping pose. Create the outline with a rectangle shape for the body and cone shapes for the legs and arms. Carefully draw the head.

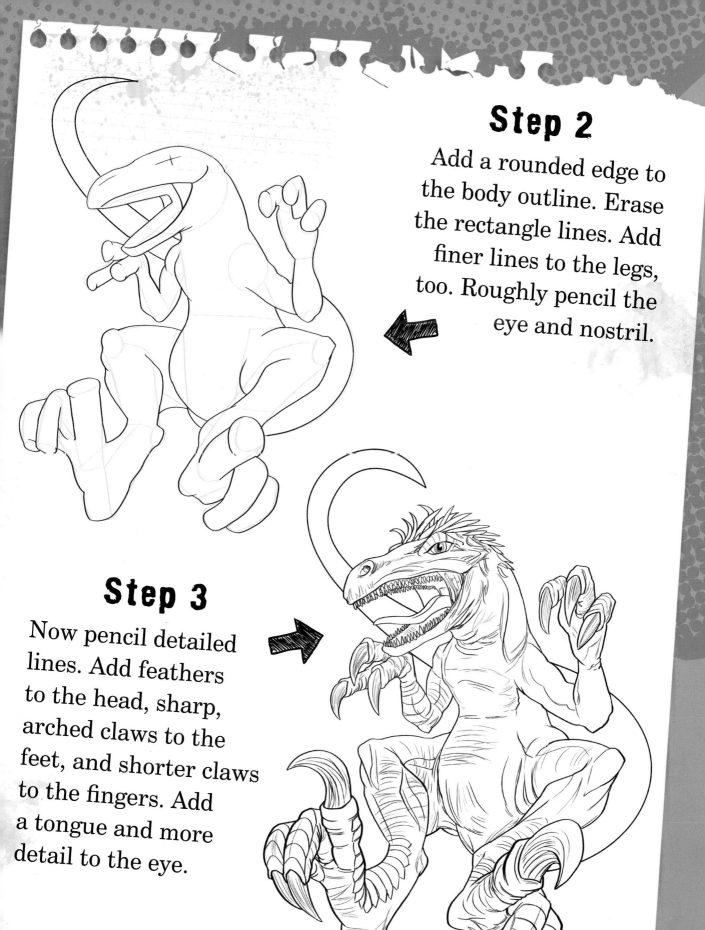

Step 2

Add a rounded edge to the body outline. Erase the rectangle lines. Add finer lines to the legs, too. Roughly pencil the eye and nostril.

Step 3

Now pencil detailed lines. Add feathers to the head, sharp, arched claws to the feet, and shorter claws to the fingers. Add a tongue and more detail to the eye.

Step 4

Add lots of fine lines to the legs, tail, arms, and head to bring the dinosaur to life. Give your creature its razor-sharp teeth.

Sharpen your skills

Try different patterns and colors. Like modern animal hunters, such as tigers, dinosaurs were probably camouflaged.

Step 5

To color your dinosaur like the one below, choose a palette of orange, brown, yellow, and cream colors. You could choose a spotted pattern like the one shown here. Color the claws with gray.

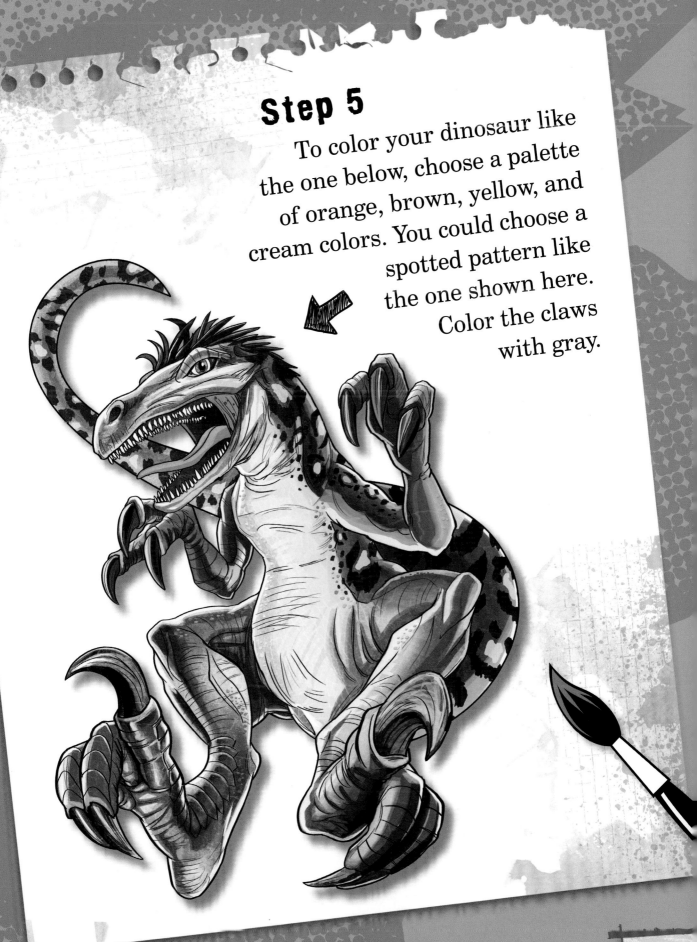

Hadrosaur

This plant-eating dinosaur is also known as the "duck-billed dinosaur" because its head is similar to that of a duck.

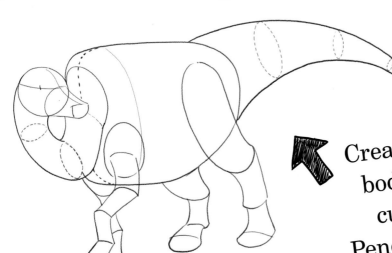

Step 1

Create a large oval for the body. Draw a long, thick, curved arch for the tail. Pencil sections for the legs and neck. Add the head.

Step 2

Draw the crest on the dinosaur's head. Pencil the eye and add toes and claws.

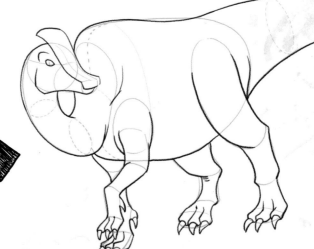

Step 3

Draw the powerful muscle lines on the body. Draw a long, ridged line along the back and tail. Add detail to the head.

Step 4

Now for the color! Remember, no one knows for certain what colors dinosaurs were. This means you can choose pretty much whatever you like! We have chosen a bright blue for the body and a light orange for the crest and ridge on the dinosaur's back. Add highlights with white paint.

Tyrannosaurus rex

Tyrannosaurus rex, or T. rex, means "king of the lizards." This deadly predator was one of the most terrifying hunters of all time.

Step 1

Use a large oval shape to create T. rex's powerful body. Pencil outlines for the head, tail, and limbs.

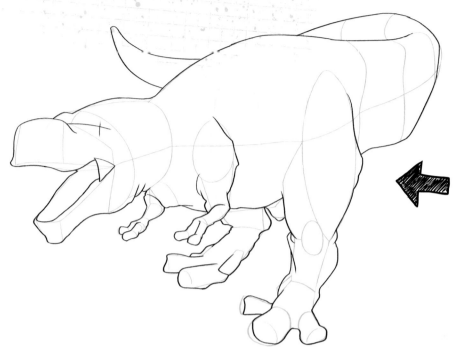

Step 2

Go over the outer lines for your dinosaur. Then erase the rough inner lines.

Step 3

Add detail by drawing the eye, nostril, and tongue. Your dinosaur should be bellowing! Pencil the killer's huge, sharp claws.

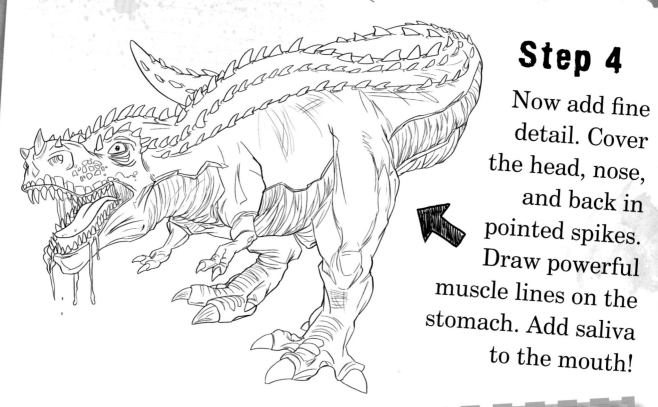

Step 4

Now add fine detail. Cover the head, nose, and back in pointed spikes. Draw powerful muscle lines on the stomach. Add saliva to the mouth!

Sharpen your skills

Try different poses and angles for the head.

Step 5

Now for the really fun part! Color your T. rex a strong purple. Use this all over its back, arms, legs, and tail. On the underside of the jaw, body, and tail, choose a bright yellow. Use the same color for the eyes and snout. Add highlights with white paint. For the final detail, paint the saliva a yellow-white!

Stegosaurus

This spine-covered dinosaur was huge, but its brain was only the size of a walnut!

Step 1

Draw a large, rounded body shape. Add cone shapes for the legs and diamond shapes for the spines.

Step 2

Trace a stronger line over the body outline. Then erase the rough inner lines.

Step 3

Pencil finer detailed lines to the spines. Add the eye, nostril, and claws. Don't forget the spikes on the tail.

Step 4

Choose a gray-blue for the body, and purple for the underbelly and legs. Bright purple and orange spines tell predators to stay away!

Deinonychus

This is a deadly killer! Deinonychus was armed with a huge claw on each of its feet, which could turn 90 degrees to rip through flesh!

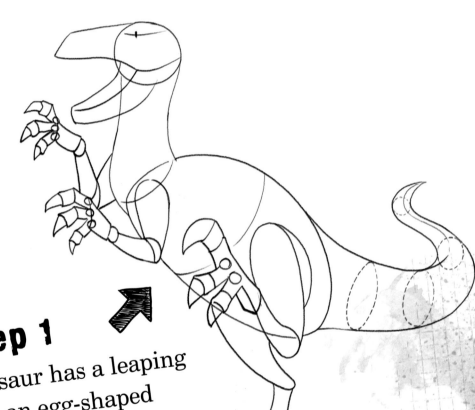

Step 1

Your dinosaur has a leaping pose. Use an egg-shaped outline for the body and smaller ovals for the legs and arms. Add the head, tail, and claws.

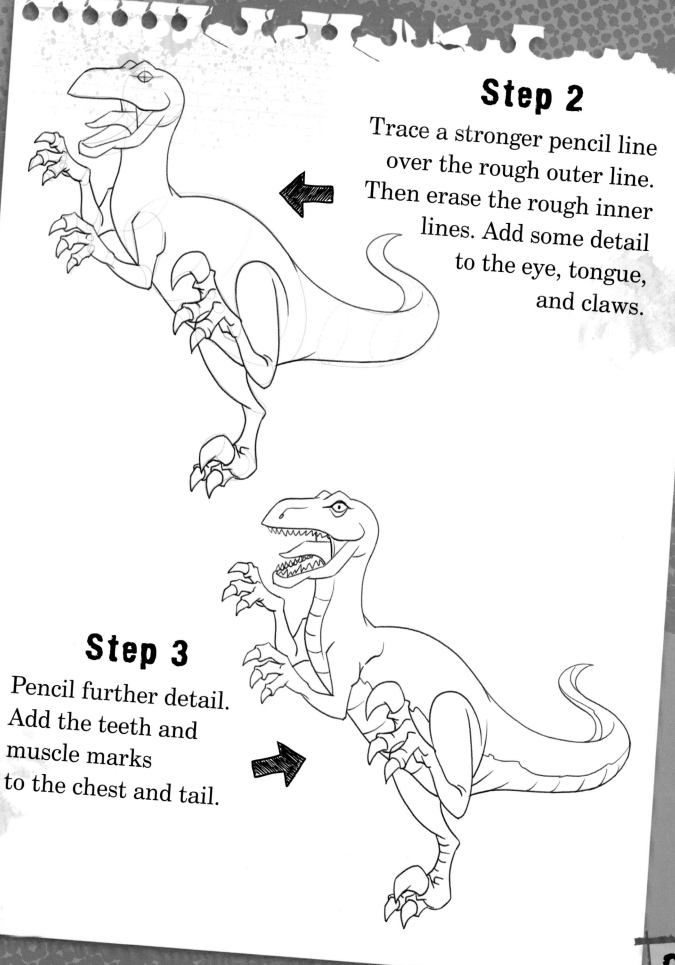

Step 2

Trace a stronger pencil line over the rough outer line. Then erase the rough inner lines. Add some detail to the eye, tongue, and claws.

Step 3

Pencil further detail. Add the teeth and muscle marks to the chest and tail.

Step 4

Now add shading to the neck, head, and mouth to give depth to the drawing.

Sharpen your skills

Deinonychus was an agile hunter. Try drawing this extra pose.

It is likely that Deinonychus was camouflaged to blend in with its surroundings. Choose natural colors such as orange-brown and beige for the body. Flashes of dark purple can be used for a pattern on the head, back, and tail. Don't forget to color the deadly claws jet black!

Megalosaurus

Another fearsome hunter, Megalosaurus was an enormous killer. This predator stalked its prey, then rushed out to attack with a crushing bite from its powerful jaws.

Step 1

Create a running pose for your hunter. Use large cone shapes for the powerful hind legs. Draw a huge head and a sweeping tail.

Step 2

Add finer lines to the rough outline. Then erase any unwanted lines.

Step 3

Add detail with muscle lines, sharp claws, horns on the head and face, and a tongue.

Step 4

Use a sharp pencil to draw a striped pattern on the tail, body, and arms. Add the teeth.

Sharpen your skills

You could try a zebralike pattern or even tiger stripes to add variety to your coloring stage.

Step 5

Go for dramatic color to bring this beast to life! Use bright purple for the back and face, and a blue for the arms and legs. A dark gray for the stripes will make them pop out from the purple. Give the dinosaur a gray mark around its eye and fill with yellow. Use white paint for highlights and the claws.

More Dinosaurs

If you've loved drawing Manga dinosaurs, try some more!

Ankylosaurus

This armored dinosaur could deliver a deadly blow with its clubbed tail.

Apatosaurus

This large, plant-eating dinosaur had a very long neck and tail.

Oviraptor

This was
a birdlike
dinosaur. It
may even have
had feathers!

Triceratops

Armed with three horns
on its head and a "shield"
on its neck, the
plant-eater
Triceratops
could take
on T. rex,
and win!

Glossary

agile (A-jul) Able to move with ease.

armored (AR-merd) Having a protective covering over the body.

bellowing (BEH-loh-ing) Making a very loud noise that can be heard from far away.

camouflaged (KA-muh-flahjd) Patterned or colored to blend in with the surroundings.

crest (KREST) A structure on a creature's head.

depth (DEPTH) To make something look three dimensional. Not flat.

detail (dih-TAYL) The small, fine lines that are used to add important features to a drawing, such as eyes, horns, and spikes.

erase (ih-RAYS) To remove.

limbs (LIMZ) Arms and legs.

nostrils (NOS-trulz) The openings on the head or face, through which air is breathed.

outline (OWT-lyn) A very simple line that provides the shape for a drawing.

palette (PA-lit) A range of colors.

plunderer (PLUN-der-er) Someone or something that takes or steals with force.

pose (POHZ) The way something or someone stands.

predator (PREH-duh-ter) A creature that hunts other creatures for food.

prehistoric (pree-his-TOR-ik) Before history was written.

prey (PRAY) A creature that is hunted and eaten by others.

ridged (RIJD) An uneven surface that is raised higher than the areas surrounding it.

saliva (suh-LY-vuh) Spit.

shading (SHAYD-ing) Creating lots of lines to add shadow and depth to a drawing.

snout (SNOWT) The nose of a creature.

Further Reading

Amberlyn, J. C. *Drawing Manga Animals, Chibis and Other Adorable Creatures*. New York: Watson-Guptill, 2009.

Giannotta, Andrés Bernardo. *How to Draw Manga*. Mineola, NY: Dover Publications, 2010.

Hart, Christopher. *Kids Draw Big Book of Everything Manga*. New York: Watson-Guptill, 2009.

Nishida, Masaki. *Drawing Manga Dinosaurs*. How to Draw Manga. New York: PowerKids Press, 2007.

Websites

Due to the changing nature of Internet links, PowerKids Press has developed an online list of websites related to the subject of this book. This site is updated regularly. Please use this link to access the list: www.powerkidslinks.com/ltdm/dino/

Index

A

adding details, 6–7, 9, 13, 15–16, 18–19, 21, 25
adding highlights, 13, 17, 27
Ankylosaurus, 28
Apatosaurus, 28

B

Brachiosaurus, 8–11

C

colors, 5, 7, 10–11, 13, 17, 23, 27

D

Deinonychus, 20–23
depth, 22

E

Eoraptor, 8–11
erasing, 5, 9, 15, 18, 21, 25

H

Hadrosaur, 12–13

M

meat-eaters, 8–11, 14–17, 19–28
Megalosaurus, 24–27

O

outlines, 8–9, 14, 18, 20, 25
Oviraptor, 29

P

painting, 5, 7, 10–11, 13, 17, 23, 27
plant-eaters, 6–7, 12–13, 18–19, 28–29
poses, 8, 20, 24

S

shading, 7, 22
shapes, 6, 8, 14, 18, 20, 24
Stegosaurus, 18–19

T

Triceratops, 29
Tyrannosaurus rex, 14–17